COARSE FISH AND FLOAT
FISHING GENERALLY

BY

H. CHOLMONDELEY-PENNELL

COARSE FISH AND FLOAT FISHING GENERALLY.

TACKLE.

HOOKS.

In every description of float-fishing, as in trolling and fly-fishing, though in a somewhat lesser degree, the hook plays the part of Hamlet, and although having already dealt with this subject *in extenso* in Vol. I. pp. 4-33, and in the present Vol. pp. 74-7 in reference to trolling hooks, I do not purpose now to go into what may be called the *rationale* of hook making as applicable to float-fishing especially, the arguments in one case practically hold good in another.

What is the best hook? The hook that kills best with the artificial fly will evidently, so far as killing powers go, catch the most fish with the worm or gentle. The only points in which some slight modification of the practical application of the principles alluded to may be necessary in the case of float-fishing are the length of the shanks and turned and needle-eyed hooks. The latter present few of the advantages which the fly-fisher, having regard to his special art, may recognise in them, and the former—that is the length of the shank—is one entirely of convenience, depending upon the nature of the bait used, and the necessity of concealing the whole of the shank, as compared with the importance of missing the smallest number of bites. It is almost a self-evident proposition that a long-shanked hook of the same size and shaped bend will have greater penetrating power than a hook with a shorter shank.

In order to arrive at this conclusion without any complicated process of reasoning out the mechanical argument it is only necessary to apply a sort of *reductio ad absurdum*, and consider what would be the actual power of a hook if the shank were reduced to the same length as the point. Evidently it would possess no penetrating power whatever. Extend the same principle to a hook with a shank slightly longer than the point, and you have a proportionate increase of hooking power, double it again, you get another increase and so on.

For reasons already stated I believe that my bend of hook, shown in the annexed plate, fig. 1, will be found far the most killing for all sorts of bottom fishing. The length of shank has been especially calculated for tying artificial flies and so far as hooking powers go is, perhaps, about the perfect length.

FIG. I.—'PENNELL SNECK-BEND,' HOOKS.

In roach fishing, however, especially when paste is the bait used, a somewhat shorter shank is probably advisable. But let there be no mistake, the convenience in more readily covering the shank with the bait is only obtained at the expense of an equivalent amount of hooking, that is killing, power. For all sorts of worm-fishing where the shank of the hook can be readily concealed the use of the full length of shank is strongly recommended. The simplest way to shorten the shanks of any of these hooks is with a small pair of pliers or in an impromptu vice formed at the joint of a pair of scissors.

In heavy fishing, where hooks larger than those shown in the engraving are used, my old bend of hooks—diagrams of which, as also of the ordinary round bend hooks, are appended —may be employed. It will be seen from the plate, fig. 2, that the two bends of hooks are numbered in different ways. My own are numbered from 1, which is probably the smallest size that will often be required in float-fishing, up to 10, the largest, suitable for barbelling and other exceptionally heavy work.

Whenever sizes of hooks are given in the following pages it is these numbers that are referred to.

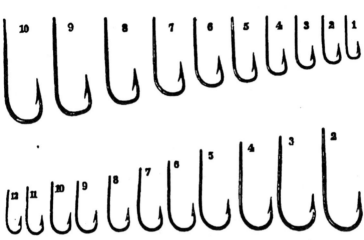

FIG. 2.—'PENNELL OLD BEND,' AND 'ROUND BEND.'

The 'sliced-hook' (*vide* cut) might be found advantageous for some sorts of fishing, such as barbelling with the lob-worm tail or fishing with the natural grasshopper, or shrimp bait, where it is desirable to prevent the bait slipping down the hook shank. I think it might be used with advantage also in almost all sorts of sea fishing with bait.

GUT.

Such observations as I am able to offer on the subject of gut and hair, having reference to the choice of methods of staining, knotting, &c., will be found at pp. 33-47 Vol. I. I do not, therefore, attempt to recapitulate them here. As regards the

FIG. 3.—'SLICED' HOOK.

REEL AND RUNNING-LINE,

the same remark applies, and I would merely say here that, setting aside such special departments as ledgering for barbel,

where an extra strong heavy line is required, and Nottingham
fishing, the disciples of which pride themselves on a wonderfully light line of undressed silk, the best sort of running-line
that I am acquainted with for every purpose is one of the
finest possible dressed silk of the thickness of ordinary stout
sewing thread, which is both perfect in manipulation and of
great strength. I have one of these lines before me now that
has gone through a fair amount of work during the past season,
both with float, fly, and worm-fishing for trout, for which latter
purpose it is especially suitable, and I find that one yard of the
end which has had all the wear is still capable of lifting a dead
weight of 6 lbs. The price is 2s. 6d. for 20 yards, or 12s. 6d.
for 100 yards, it is manufactured and sold by Watson and Sons,
308 High Holborn, London, under the designation of ' Braided
Waterproof Lines, No. H.' G, the next size larger, is 3s. per
score yards, and so on down to A, which is a strong salmon
line. Either E or D would be suited to ledgering for barbel or
other heavy work. With this line also, and a rod with stiff rings
I can easily throw a light tackle and float 15 or 20 yards, and
very likely more, but it will not, of course, 'float' so well as
undressed line. I have never yet tried how far I could throw it,
but I have repeatedly thrown it the distance in question. This
facility of casting is a very important part of a float-fisher's
equipment, as it enables him to command any part of a
pond or river which it is practically likely he may require to
reach.

The Nottingham line used with, and especially suitable to
the Nottingham tackle, is equally suitable to *almost* every kind
of float fishing (except jack fishing). It is made of pure undressed silk and combines great strength with the utmost lightness and fineness, being about, in fact, the thickness of the
dressed line above described. Extreme lightness is desirable
to give it flotation, where, as in the Nottingham style, long
casts are made or the float travels a long way down stream, and
there is sometimes as much as thirty or forty yards of line in
the water at the same time. It must also be free from kinking

proclivities and run very easily or it will not pass through the rod rings with sufficient freedom.

A line of this kind was supplied to me by Mr. Baily, the well-known Nottingham troller, and it fulfils admirably all these conditions. It is composed of six or eight of the finest possible strands of silk plaited somewhat in a square shape. A hundred yards of it weigh exactly three-eighths of an ounce, and yet, notwithstanding this extreme fineness, I find it will lift a dead weight of between six and seven pounds, which is far beyond the strain it is ever likely to be subjected to. In fact, for all kinds of bottom-fishing this will be found a truly excellent line, but care must be taken to get the real thing. Still, for some sorts of fishing the advantage will probably be thought in practice to rest with the dressed silk line which I have already recommended, but there are many others, I am free to admit, in which the undressed silk from its greater lightness and floating qualities would have the votes in its favour, and in securing a float-fisher's outfit it would be well to have a running line of each sort. The price of the Nottingham line is 5s. per 100 yards of the plaited quality described ; the twisted description being 2s. 6d. per 100 yards.

Whenever a reel is necessary, and I confess I seldom care about fishing of any kind without one, any ordinary check reel, such as can be obtained at every tackle shop, and not too large, will answer the purpose, observing that it is desirable the 'check' should be as light as possible, as if it is too heavy it will not allow a small fish to carry out the line with sufficient ease.

RODS.

What observations on rods, in addition to those previously given, may be desirable in this division of my subject will be probably more conveniently distributed under the headings to which they more especially pertain. 'Combination rods' have been frequently invented which, by a transposition of tops, butts, and middle joints can be made to fulfil almost any *rôle*—

both in fly, float-fishing, and trolling—more *or less* satisfactorily. Of these combination rods, one of the most ingenious that I have met with is the so-called *Multum in parvo* rod made by Mr. James Ogden, of Cheltenham. I cannot say, however, that my experience hitherto leads me to have any great faith in rods which combine such a great variety of characters. The convenience of carrying is certainly a point in their favour. In regard to ferrules, splicings, &c., I may observe that the joint fastening which is best for the fly rod and the jack rod is best also for every other sort of rod, and that anybody who henceforward buys a rod with the old joint and reel fastenings deserves to have what he certainly will get, an imperfect and defective weapon. The reel fastening already recommended for trolling and fly-rods is simply perfection, and, therefore, difficult as it is to prophesy what future discoveries may *not* bring forth, in this case, at least, we may assume to have approached finality. When an invention fulfils every demand which the most *exigeant* can imagine, there is little left for future inventors to experiment upon.

Before quitting the subject of rods, let me recommend that for every description, whether trolling, fly-fishing, or float-fishing, the rings should be stiff, upright rings, although for the last-named object—float-fishing—the rings may be very much smaller than those required for trolling. Such rings made of steel need be no heavier than the ordinary flapping brass rings, commonly sold at the tackle shops, which are subject to innumerable drawbacks—the first being the habit of sticking at some point or other of the rod and so preventing the free passage of the line, the second is their coming off altogether, leaving a 'ghastly gap' in which the line loops itself.

CREELS.

As the bank fisher has generally some *impedimenta* to stow away, and being more or less stationary, prefers setting down his basket to carrying it constantly on his shoulder, he would probably prefer the ordinary wicker-work creel to the waterproof bag of the trout-fisher, which, however, when empty weighs next to nothing.

It is bad enough to have to carry an empty panier when it is a light one, but when it is a heavy one it is more than human nature can stand. Some of the best and most recent improvements in the matter of fish-carriers, whether bag or basket, will be found figured in Vol. I. pp. 93–7.

LANDING NETS.

A gaff is rarely of any use in float-fishing, as the fish caught seldom run of sufficient size to make its application necessary or, indeed, possible.

A landing net with a fairly long handle will, however, be found an indispensable adjunct where the fish run anything over half-a-pound, and even under that weight, especially in the case of fish that are not 'leather-mouthed,' the presence of a landing net will frequently prevent loss. The handiest net for all sorts of fishing that I know of is that already described and here repeated to save the trouble of reference. The mode of fixing the arms of the net combines the utmost simplicity with efficiency and strength ; the two arms can be separated in a moment, when they lie flat together and roll up in the net like a walking-stick. The net itself should always be made of oiled silk, both for durability and also to prevent the hooks catching, as they are apt to do, in the fibres of ordinary string or twine nets. A net of the measurements given is the most suitable for trout fishing with the fly, where the fish do not run very large. It would be found large enough for landing any fish up to $1\frac{1}{2}$ lbs. or probably 2 lbs. with a little management. For barbelling and chub or bream fishing it would be advisable to have one at least fifteen or sixteen inches between the points. In order to make a net of this size carry well, however, the supporting shoulder cord will have to be proportionately lengthened and the butt of the handle leaded, to prevent, in the first place, the net touching under the arm of the fisherman, and, secondly, overbalancing itself and falling out of the carrier altogether. The necessity of this would doubtless be diminished, if not nearly obviated, by the suggested alteration in the net handle that I

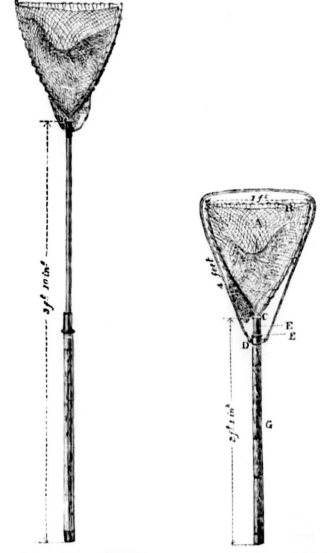

FIG. 1.—LANDING-NET EXTENDED.   FIG. 2.—LANDING-NET CLOSED.

have already made, namely, that the catch-rim against which the suspender is supported should be put right up at the top of the ferrule, at C, in fact, instead of at D (*vide* diagram 2), thus adding materially to the balance as well as to the general convenience of the whole thing.

It would then, I believe, be an absolutely perfect net. The net is the production of Messrs. Hardy Bros., Alnwick, and the handle and carrier that of Mrs. Williams, of Great Queen Street, Lincoln's Inn Fields. I have merely performed the part of mortar in uniting the two bricks of the edifice. But, no doubt, after this book is published, at least these two tacklemakers will make the whole net complete as shown.

In landing a fish, the net should be kept as much out of sight as possible until the moment of using it, when it should be rapidly, but steadily, passed under the fish from *below and behind*; the movement of getting the fish into the net being, therefore, a lifting and 'sweeping' movement, so to speak.

FLOATS, SHOT, AND SUNDRIES.

FLOATS.

Floats are amongst the items in fishermen's equipment which have also, I think, been carried as near the point of perfection as possible. Floats of the most fascinating shapes, of every size, colour, and combination of cork and quill, can be obtained in the tackle shops. For the sake of convenience, I have had half-a-dozen of the most useful shapes engraved.

No. 1 is made of cork with a porcupine quill running through the middle. It has the merit of being one of the strongest possible forms of float, sightly, and at the same time a 'good steady carrier,' in fact, the float fisher will find that made of different shapes and sizes, there is no float which can be more satisfactorily used in the greatest number of circumstances. And this observation applies as well to pond as to river fishing.

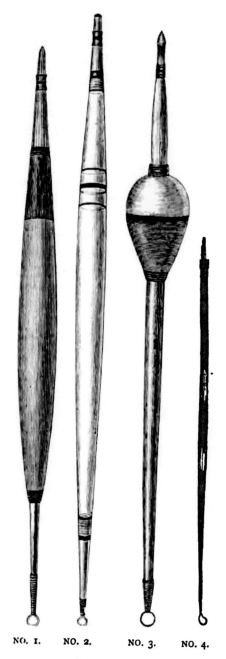

No. 2 is made entirely of tapered quill. It is beautiful as a work of art, and with ivory tips exercises a decided fascination upon the minds of many roach fishers, by whom, indeed, it is most frequently patronised.

No. 3 is a variation of No. 1, the central shaft of it being again of porcupine quill, and the enlarged portion of cork. This is a float especially suited to perch-fishing in lakes and ponds, and

' Should you rove for a perch
with a pink or minnow,'

will carry the latter very satisfactorily.

No. 4 is a very small-sized plain porcupine quill, and can be used of the size shown in the drawing with advantage where the very finest fishing is necessary, as the line requires to be only very lightly shotted to cock the float, and at the slightest bite it is taken under water, being also so small and unattractive in colour as to disturb the water very little. For river

NO. 1.   NO. 2.   NO. 3.   NO. 4.

fishing, however, where there is any current to speak of, No. 4 will be found practically useless, as the slightest touch, whether from weed or gravel, or even the sweep of the current itself will suffice to carry it under.

For ordinary float fishing the four descriptions indicated will be found all that the most fastidious can require. Of float No. 1 it would be desirable to keep three sizes, one larger and one smaller than the pattern. Where it is necessary to fish deep in a strong stream, it is also necessary to have a good many shot on the line to carry the bait with sufficient rapidity to the bottom, and to prevent the stream unduly 'bagging' the line. For this purpose it is, of course, also necessary to have a float of corresponding carrying powers, and I think that even a fourth size of No. 1, a still larger size than those already mentioned—making altogether four sizes of No. 1—ought to be kept by the float fisher in case of emergency. Nos. 2 and 3 are also made both smaller and larger, but on the whole, I think the two sizes represented will be found most convenient.

So much for ordinary floats; I now come to the extraordinary floats.

No. 5 is a smaller size of the Nottingham or travelling float—that is, the float used in what is known as the 'Nottingham style' of float fishing. Its peculiarities, it will be noticed, consist first in the fact that it is bow-shaped instead of straight, and that the bottom loop is at right angles with, instead of perpendicular to, the shaft, and that, in lieu of the ordinary quill or gutta-percha cap, there

NO. 5.

is a small projecting brass loop through which the line can run with perfect freedom. The float, therefore, travels up and down the line, and at the point where it is intended it should rest, that is, as the expression is, at the right 'depth,' a small piece of gut or line is knotted in the running line above the float, with the result that, of course, when the line is running downwards through the rings to this point, the float remains stationary. It is thus that the Nottingham fisher is enabled to make such long casts. As the line is drawn back out of the water, the float naturally slips down the line until it is stopped by the shot, and in this position forms an additional weight at the point where weight is most essential to enable a long cast to be made with ease. Having drawn in his line up to the 'sticking' point, i.e. the transverse piece of gut or quill—which may be the length of his rod or even more above the float—he makes his cast to ten or twenty, or, perhaps, even twenty-five yards, as the case may be, and giving line freely, the shot carry the bait down to the bottom of the river or pond to the depth which has been already carefully plummed, leaving the float as usual on the surface. This is, however, only one of the two great advantages of this kind of float. The second is the fact that in striking the fish from whatever distances, especially long ones, the stroke has not to overcome the *vis inertiæ* of the float before it can reach the mouth of the fish. This is a point of great importance, and one without which fishing in the Nottingham style, that is, covering long reaches of water at great distances from the fisher- man, could not be successfully carried out.

No. 6, the last float in the list, is probably still more entitled to be called extraordinary. It is called the 'electric-float,' and is supposed to be luminous at the top, so that in night fishing it is always readily perceptible.

NO. 6.

N.B.—I don't assert that the float actually fulfils these con- ditions, but they are the specialties claimed for it. What the object of the circular notch round the upper part of the cork may be, except to hold the little indiarubber ring now shown about half-an-inch above it, I am únable to explain, and if it is intended to hold it, I can furnish no explanation of why the ring should be placed at such an unusual part of the float, unless it be to make, so to speak, a higher stand for the lamp.

Given, however, the fact that one can see the float in the dark, the next point that arises is whether the fish can see the bait, or if they can, are likely to bite at it at that part of the twenty-four hours. I must confess again to not having tried the experiment practically, and, therefore, in summing-up these few remarks on the 'electric-float,' all I can say is that if it is not 'true' it is at any rate 'new.'

Besides the floats shown in the engravings, there is still another very useful kind of float which I had overlooked. It is made the lower part of porcupine and the upper of goose or swan quill. In consequence of the amount of air contained in the upper portion it is an excellent carrier of its size, and, therefore, worthy of an honourable place in the float-fisher's table of precedence.

Another float, which, if not extraordinary, can certainly hardly be called ordinary, has recently been invented by Mr. Gillet, the well-known tackle-maker of Fetter Lane. It is a float which *cocks itself*, and is called 'Gillet's self-cocking float.' It is strongly recommended by Mr. Greville Fennell in his 'Book of the Roach.' After stating his fruitless efforts to circumvent the roach of certain ponds, he says :—

We then bethought us to imitate as nearly as possible the action of the slow descending particles of loose ground-bait thrown in to allure the fish and instead of using a shotted line, which sank rapidly, and consequently unnaturally reaches the bottom long before the ground-bait, we removed all the shot, and placing sufficient in the quill, we found we had achieved a success, as it permitted the bait to sink by its own gravity. The effect was immediate and decided. . . . This method is wonderfully destructive to dace when the house-fly is used.

This float is weighted so as to swim the proper depth as weighted by the line, hook, and bait, 'when' says the gentleman who describes it, 'it may be regulated to detect the finest bite.' This writer also says that he has been very successful with it in mill tails amongst the dace, baited with a single gentle or red-worm, when with the ordinary shotted float he could not succeed in catching them. The self-cocking apparatus consists of a drop or two of quicksilver enclosed in the end of the transparent tapered quill.

The object of this is to dispense with the

SHOT OR LEAD WIRE,

which latter, intended not only to cock the float, but also to carry the bait to the bottom, are best used large rather than numerous and, with the exception of the lowest one, distributed, in pond fishing, as far away from the bait as possible. In river fishing it is necessary to get the bait quickly to the bottom and to keep the current from lifting it off again. Consequently it becomes necessary to get the shot somewhat closer together on the lower part of the line. The shot should be heavy enough to submerge the float up to the, as I may call it, high water mark, generally about three-quarters of the way up, but in many cases the float swims better and bites can be more readily perceived when the float is sunk rather over the mark in question.

Some float-fishers instead of using split shot, with the annoyance of having to bite them on with your teeth when they have to be attached, and cut them out with your penknife at the risk of the line when they have to be detached, use a soft leaden wire, the invention, I believe, and, at any rate, manufacture of the Manchester Cotton Spinning Co., 51 Corporation Street, Manchester, which can be coiled with great facility round the line with the fingers and uncoiled again as soon as it is wished to alter the 'swim of the float,' or the float itself. An illustration of the wire coiled on gut line is annexed.[1]

---

[1] The actual leaden wire, of which samples have been furnished to me by the Company, is about as thick as the finest twine. It is sold by them in hanks or knots of 15 yards, price one shilling the hank. The Manchester Company has

This fine wire is, however, more suitable for fine tackle and very light fishing than for floats requiring to be heavily leaded. The piece of lead coil represented is about equal to two No. 4 shot, and would cock a porcupine quill float about half as long again as No. 4. For very light tackle it has however, I think, several advantages, one of which is that there is no danger of nipping the line, as is the case with shot which have been squeezed tightly on. All that is necessary to coil the wire is to lay a pin parallel with the gut, twisting the wire round both ; and then, after withdrawing the pin tightening the coils as much as requisite by twisting them with the finger and thumb.

To return : after the float naturally comes

THE PLUMMET,

LEAD-WIRE FOR WEIGHTING FLOAT-LINES.

which is essential to ascertain the depth of the water and the distance from the bottom (or on the bottom, as the case may be) at which it is desired that the bait should travel. The best of the old-fashioned plummets is simply a sheet of soft lead wound round the line above the hook in the position shown in the engraving (fig. 1). An improvement upon it was, however, exhibited last year by Mr. Thomas Hines, of Norwich. The action of it will be under-

also sent me samples of a very fine soft copper wire for lapping over pike tackle, finishing off top ring fastenings, &c., and other analogous purposes. They have been for many years manufacturing a superfine ' thrown silk,' as contrasted with ' floss' silk, on the one hand and sewing silk on the other, for whipping hooks, flies, &c. An immense comfort will be found in tackle-making, from the use of this silk, which, though exceedingly fine is strong enough to admit of considerable strain without breaking. The finest and purest silk of all, however, is that used by the gold twist makers of Little Britain, London, in their manufacture of gold lace for buttons, uniforms, &c. For ' waxing' this and other kinds of silk, a very small piece of cobblers' wax about as big as a No. 1 shot and rolled between the finger and thumb will be found a great convenience. When used in larger lumps it is difficult, especially in cold weather, to keep it at the necessary temperature.

stood by a glance at the illustrative diagram (fig. 2). The thumb being pressed upon the point *b*, the loop, *a*, is pushed

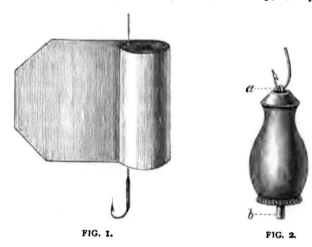

FIG. 1.   FIG. 2.

upwards by a spring, the hook passed through in the position shown, and kept afterwards in its place by the downward action of the liberated spring.

A ROD REST.

A *desideratum* which will add greatly to the comfort both of the bank and punt fisher, has been lately patented by Messrs. C. L. Matthews & Co., No. 1A Wynyatt Street, St. John Street Road, London, E.C., under the name of the 'Adjustable Fishing Rod Holder.' This invention, of which diagrams are appended, is obtainable from Messrs. Matthews, wholesale and retail. The rod holder in black iron costs 1*s.* 6*d.* ; the boat clip, the same ; or better finished and nickel plated twice as much. Fig. 1 shows the rod holder as it would appear when stuck upright in the bank. Fig. 2, the same stuck in a perpendicular bank. Fig. 3, the boat clip, by which it can be fixed to the side of the punt. Fig. 4 shows the adjustment of the boat clip with the rod holders in position. The inventor claims the following advantages amongst others for his rod holder :—

1. The rod can be fixed so that the butt end comes to the edge of the water, thus bringing the full length of the rod into use.

2. The rod holder can be adjusted so as to fish when the water is bank high or some feet below.

3. The rod holder can be stuck into the sheer face of a high bank (fig. 2), and the point of the rod depressed as near the water as desired.

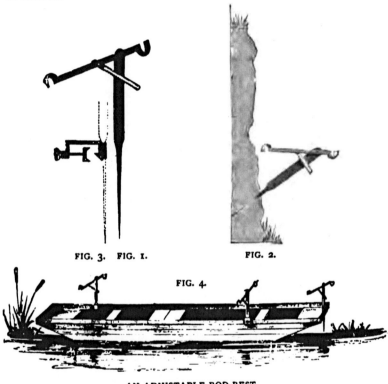

FIG. 3.   FIG. 1.   FIG. 2.

FIG. 4.

AN ADJUSTABLE ROD-REST.

4. The rod is so held that instantly a bite is seen one can strike as freely as though it had been held in the hand all the time.

5. The rod holder can be adjusted to any angle without taking it out of the ground.

6. In boat fishing, the same advantages attend the use of the rod holder as when fishing from the bank. All anglers know how awkward it is to have the rod lying across the boat.

7. When using the rod holder, there is no danger of losing the rod ; it cannot roll or tip from the boat or bank, no fish can run off with it, and the pressure of wind only makes it hold tighter.

8. The rod holder holds equally well long or short, thick or thin, light or heavy rods ; in fact, it is so adapted that the greater the strain the greater the security.

9. The rod holder when not in use will close up in such a small compass that it may easily be carried in the bag, basket, or pocket, its weight being but a few ounces.

Float Caps.—The best float caps are quill, as unless the outside silk lapping gives way they are practically indestructible.

Not so gutta percha caps, which after keeping a certain time lose all the qualities of elasticity and almost of cohesion. I have before me a box of gutta percha caps which have been some years in stock and they break to pieces merely on being taken hold of by the fingers.

Tackle Varnish.—The appearance as well as the durability of all fishing tackle is enhanced by the addition of a coat of varnish over the silk lapping. A receipt for the best varnish for this purpose with which I am acquainted is given at page 17.

Tackle Vice.—A vice which can be attached to the table and containing a hook for loop-tying and other incidental purposes will be found a luxury to those who make their own tackle.

FISHING PLIERS.

Fishing Pliers.—Mr. R. B. Marston has invented a most excellent combination of the above. It is so useful and complete that I append a diagram of it. It contains :—

1st, a strong pair of pliers.

2nd, shot splitter.

3rd, wire or hook cutter.

4th, by an ingenious contrivance in the centre of the joint between the two arms, a cutter for extra thick wire.

5th, screw-driver.

6th, a sort of gimlet for boring broken joints out of ferrules.

The pliers can be obtained of Messrs. Barron and Wilson, King William Street, Strand.

'THE FISHERMAN'S KNIFE.'

For all sorts of float- as well as fly-fishing, a pocket-knife with a 'disgorger' blade that can be carried anywhere, and

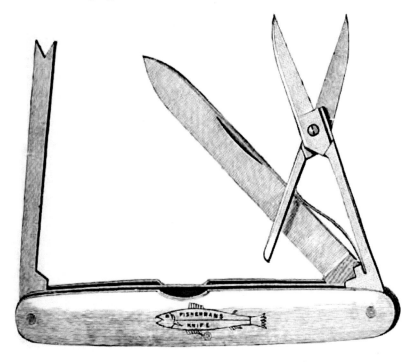

opened readily from any position, is a great, I might almost say, indispensable convenience.

The 'Fisherman's Knife,' as it has been christened, figured in the engraving, a descendant of my other knife rechristened the 'Troller's Knife,' contains all the outdoor requisites in a thoroughly compact form. It is manufactured and sold by Messrs. Watson and Sons, 308 High Holborn, London, at the very modest price of 6*s.* 6*d.*

A very convenient general tackle-box is sold by Messrs. Chevalier, Bowness and Bowness, of 230 Strand. This box, which is made in japanned tin, is designed to carry a complete stock of tackle, as well for the fly-fisher as the troller, &c.[1]

---

[1] Depth, 11 inches; length, 14 inches; width, 10 inches. In the lid are compartments, containing traces, casts, &c. Two trays for artificial baits; one tray for salmon flies, and one tray with four partitions for trout flies. There is a large space underneath the bottom tray for reels, lines, and tackle generally. The price of the tackle box is three guineas.

Lightning Source UK Ltd.
Milton Keynes UK
UKOW051859110213

206132UK00001B/275/P